G000043528

miniaturefeasts

First published in Great Britain in 2006 by
The Book Guild Ltd.
Pavilion View
19 New Road
Brighton, East Sussex
BN1 1UF

Photography, art direction & design by Steve McCallum at S.M.A.K.

Printed and bound in Singapore under the supervision of
MRM Graphics Ltd, Winslow, Bucks.

A catalogue record of this book is available in the British Library

ISBN 1 84624 025 5

miniaturefeasts

michael harwood

photography by steve mccallum

Book Guild Publishing
Sussex, England

ACKNOWLEDGEMENTS

Kath at Sneek

Bill's Produce Store at The Depot

Steamer Trading

Abode

JBPR

Absolute Brighton

The Fish Shop at Kensington Place

Jereboams, Holland Park

To Al, Steve and Jo

contents

introduction

Throwing a great party is a bit like mixing a good cocktail: you need to have all the right ingredients and know how to mix them. The most important ingredient is of course a crowd of your favourite people, but if you want to throw a party to remember (and who doesn't?) you'll need to give plenty of thought to the music, the lighting, the drinks and of course the food.

Gone are the days when you could get away with a bowl of kettle chips and a cheese and pineapple hedgehog; no, these days a really great bash needs food with a bit of attitude, food that can stand its ground against a traditional sit-down meal. After all, quite often nibbles aren't just the warm-up act for dinner, they *are* dinner.

Whatever the reason for your party, be it a big bash or an intimate soirée, *Miniature Feasts* will help you to design a menu to wow friends and family, leaving a lasting impression of you as a generous and creative host. With all that new-found confidence you'll be throwing parties for birthdays, anniversaries, even for no good reason at all, and the one thing they'll have in common is great food and good hospitality.

planning your menu

So, the date is set and the invites have gone out, the next thing to organise is the menu.

First of all you need to assess what kind of bash you're having and to help you do this I've organised *Miniature Feasts* into five separate chapters:

PRE-DINNER has light bites, suitable for nibbles with drinks, nothing too filling and certainly nothing that will spoil your dinner.

AFTER DARK is an altogether more sultry affair with slightly more substantial nibbles that will see you and your guests through an evening of champagne and cocktail sipping. Some of these miniature feasts require a little more preparation but are designed to be made in relatively small numbers and many have tips for how to prepare ahead.

FEEDING A CROWD will help to take the hassle out of feeding the masses. The emphasis here is on tasty finger food that has a high yield. Each of these recipes makes larger-scale catering a breeze and is designed to be low maintenance for the host or hostess. All of the recipes involve a certain amount of prior preparation but can be finished at the last minute and served to an eagerly waiting crowd.

FAMILY FAVOURITES is a collection of recipes based on all our favourite comfort foods but miniaturised. These recipes are particularly handy for big family gatherings where there will be lots of children and you don't want to resort to the usual 'kiddie fodder'. This is real food that will appeal to the young and not so young alike.

SOMETHING SWEET is a great way to finish an evening and a final sugar rush always comes as a pleasant surprise to guests who have been grazing on savoury treats. All the recipes in this chapter are prepared ahead of time and require only a little attention just before serving.

Once you have decided what kind of gathering you're having, the next thing to do is assess how much time you have and start building your menu. The chapters are simply a suggestion, so don't be afraid of mixing and matching the recipes. You may decide, for example, to knock up a batch of 'mini sausages with a sweet and sticky glaze' and some 'mini shepherd's pies' to keep the kids happy while the grown-ups feast on 'deep fried oysters with a shot of Bloody Mary'. The trick is to make the menu work for you and your guests.

BASICS is the section where you will find essential recipes for dips, pastry and bread dough.

A note on quantities: Most of the recipes in this book make either 12 or 24 and all are easy to halve, double or even treble.

Many people find it difficult to calculate how many items of finger food to offer their guests, so I've worked out the following formula to help:

- For pre-dinner drinks allow 4 bites per person, with a choice of 4 different items.
- For most other parties allow 5 bites per person per hour. For example, a cocktail party lasting 3 hours would require a total of 15 bites per person, with a choice of 5 different items.

If you plan to offer finger food in place of lunch or dinner, increase the number of bites per hour to 6–8 including some sweet items.

A note on special equipment: I've tried to create the recipes in this book without the need for lots of hard to find equipment. There are, however, a few pieces of equipment that are well worth investing in if you plan on making the most of this book.

- Non-stick mini muffin tins, which usually come with 12 holes.
- Shot glasses – great for serving individual trifles and prawn cocktails.
- A range of bamboo skewers and cocktail sticks.
- Dipping bowls – try looking in your local Asian supermarket for interesting ones.
- Melon baller – cheap and indispensable for that professional finish.
- A ridged grill pan – for that 'char grilled' look.
- Chinese soup spoons – a great way to serve difficult to handle food.
- Espresso cups – perfect for soup shots.
- Lots of interesting plates and platters – I always check out charity shops for unusual plates as well as my local Asian supermarket.
- A kitchen blow torch – more accurate than a grill.
- A set of plain cookie cutters.
- Non-stick baking parchment – absolutely indispensable.
- Good quality plastic storage containers – for food prepared ahead of time.

OVEN TEMPERATURES

GAS MARK	°F	°C
1	275	140
2	300	150
3	325	170
4	350	180
5	375	190
6	400	200
7	425	220
8	450	230
9	475	240

WEIGHTS

IMPERIAL	METRIC
½oz	10g
⅓oz	20g
1oz	25g
1½oz	40g
2oz	50g
2½oz	60g
3oz	75g
4oz	110g
4½oz	125g
5oz	150g
6oz	175g
7oz	200g
8oz	225g
9oz	250g
10oz	275g
12oz	350g
1lb	450g
1½lbs	700g
2lbs	900g

VOLUMES

IMPERIAL	METRIC
2floz	55ml
3floz	75ml
¼ pint	150ml
½ pint	275ml
¾ pint	425ml
1 pint	570ml
1¼ pints	725ml
1¾ pints	1 litre

OTHER MEASUREMENTS

1 cup = 240ml

¾ cup = 180ml

1 teaspoon = 5ml

1 tablespoon = 15ml

* SATURDAY NIGHT

JUDE (V) CRAIG
MARTYN SOPHIE
DAVE CHARLOTTE
LIVIA (V) HANNAH
GUS JEMIMAH
VITA STU

pre-dinner

CHEESE STRAWS

Crunchy and deeply savoury, these are just the thing to keep your guests going until dinner. For a slight twist on the following recipe, try swapping the mustard for sun-dried tomato paste, black olive tapenade or even anchovy paste.

Ingredients: ***(makes 48)***

500g pack of puff pastry at room temperature
250g strong mature Cheddar or Gruyère cheese, grated
50g Parmesan, finely grated
4 tablespoons whole grain mustard
1 tablespoon sea salt
2 eggs, beaten

Method:

Roll out the pastry to a rectangle approximately 50cm x 30cm and no more than ½cm thick. Then divide in half along the short edge.

Spread one half with the mustard and top with the grated Cheddar or Gruyère. Brush the other half with eggwash and then sandwich the two together. Brush the top with more eggwash and sprinkle with the Parmesan and sea salt. Roll out to a slightly larger rectangle to ensure that the two layers are well sealed.

Cut into strips approximately 1cm wide and gently twist each end of the strips in opposing directions to give you neatly twisted straws.

Place on a baking sheet and bake at 180°C/Gas 4 for 10–15 minutes until golden brown and crisp.

TIP: The cheese straws can be made, shaped and stored in the fridge for up to 2 days before you need them. When you are ready to serve them simply place on a baking sheet straight from the fridge and bake as directed.

CHICORY BOATS FILLED WITH BEETROOT, ORANGE AND FETA SALAD

These are simply a finger food version of one of my favourite summer salads. The chicory leaves make an excellent vehicle for a light and refreshing salad, which would otherwise need a plate and fork.

Ingredients: ***(makes 24)***

4–6 heads of chicory depending on how big they are

4 medium, cooked and peeled beetroot cut into 1cm dice

4 oranges, peeled, segmented and cut into roughly the same size dice as the beetroot

250g feta, cut into 1cm dice

1 teaspoon sherry vinegar

1 tablespoon extra virgin olive oil

Pinch sea salt

Small bunch of chives, chopped

Method:

Cut the base of each chicory head and pull away the layers of leaves with your hands. When you've done this, select 24 of the best-looking leaves and set aside.

To make the salad simply combine the other ingredients, except the feta which needs to be added at the last minute to retain its colour.

Divide among the chicory leaves and serve immediately.

BRESAOLA, WILD ROCKET AND BUFFALO MOZZARELLA ROLLS

Bresaola is thinly sliced cured fillet of beef and is a speciality of Northern Italy. Its delicious peppery flavour complements the crisp wild rocket and rich milky buffalo mozzarella brilliantly. It's widely available these days in the deli section of most good supermarkets, as is the mozzarella.

Ingredients: ***(makes 24)***

250g buffalo mozzarella

12 thin slices of bresaola

1 bunch of wild rocket, washed and patted dry on kitchen paper

Extra virgin olive oil

Sea salt

Method:

Cut the mozzarella into 4 slices and then cut each slice into 3, leaving you with 12 pieces about the size and thickness of your middle finger.

Lay out the slices of bresaola on a board and place a piece of cheese on each, followed by a few leaves of rocket, allowing the leaves to extend from the edge of the meat.

Roll up neatly and then cut in half with a sharp knife.

Drizzle the rolls with olive oil and sprinkle with a small amount of sea salt.

TIP: The rolls can be made a couple of hours ahead of time and covered with damp kitchen paper and cling film before storing in the fridge. Allow to come to room temperature before serving.

STIR-FRIED ALMONDS WITH WHOLE SPICES AND CURRY LEAVES

A million miles away from anything you'll find in a packet, these little beauties are full of complex curry flavours and are totally addictive! Don't be alarmed at the amount of salt; it's there to bring out all the other flavours and is still a fraction of the amount you'd find in a commercial product. Perfect served with a glass of ice cold beer.

Ingredients:

500g whole almonds with their skins on
½ tablespoon cumin seeds
½ tablespoon coriander seeds
½ tablespoon fennel seeds
½ tablespoon mustard seeds
1 pinch chilli flakes
2 tablespoons Maldon sea salt
Small handful curry leaves stripped from the stalk
1 tablespoon groundnut oil

Method:

In a pestle and mortar lightly crush the spices and salt.

Heat a dry wok until hot and add the spices. Stir-fry until fragrant – about 3–4 minutes, being careful not to burn them.

Next, add the nuts, curry leaves and oil and continue to stir fry until well coated and lightly browned.

Allow to cool and serve in bowls.

PINZIMONIO

A good 'pinzimonio' starts with the very best olive oil you can find, followed by a large selection of crunchy baby vegetables. It's a great thing to give your guests if you're serving a hearty meal later on. The actual word 'pinzimonio' comes from the Italian *pinzare*, to pinch, and 'monio' from *matrimonio*, marriage. By pinching and marrying the baby vegetables with extra virgin olive oil, salt and cracked black pepper one has a 'pinzimonio'.

Ingredients:
The following are just some of the vegetables you could include in your pinzimonio, but any small tender vegetables will do so long as they're no bigger than a couple of bites. Obviously you can prepare this for any number of people.

Baby carrots, peeled and leafy tops left intact
Baby asparagus spears
Vine cherry tomatoes
Radishes, scrubbed
Red chicory leaves
Baby gem leaves
Stems of purple sprouting broccoli
Cauliflower florets
Baby fennel bulbs, trimmed and split into two
Red peppers, cut into strips
Baby artichoke hearts

Method:

Place your vegetables on a platter surrounded with small bowls of extra virgin olive oil seasoned with sea salt and liberal amounts of freshly cracked black pepper.

SMASHED OLIVES

Many recipes for marinated olives result in nothing more than heavily-flavoured oil. By slightly smashing the olives with the back of a heavy knife you allow them to soak up all the great punchy flavours in the marinade. This still results in a well-flavoured oil which is worth keeping long after the olives are eaten and makes great salad dressings.

Ingredients:

500g fat juicy olives with the stone in (my preference is for green but black would work too)

Juice of 1 lemon

2 cloves garlic, squashed slightly with the skin left on

1 whole lemon, thinly sliced

2 red chillies, sliced down the middle

3 bay leaves

1 tablespoon fennel seeds

1 sprig rosemary

2 tablespoons red wine vinegar

250ml plain olive oil – *not* extra virgin

Method:

First, crush the olives individually with the back of a heavy knife and set aside.

In a heavy-based saucepan, gently warm all the other ingredients. Do not overheat.

Add the crushed olives and turn off the heat.

Carefully spoon into a sterilised jar while still warm and if necessary top up with more oil so that all the olives are covered.

The olives will keep in the unopened jar for 3 months, so long as they're submerged in oil and the jar is spotlessly clean. Once opened, refrigerate and consume within one week.

Tip: To sterilise jars simply place them in your dishwasher with no other items and wash on the hottest setting. When the cycle is finished do not touch the insides of the jars, handle with a clean cloth only until they are sealed.

SWISS CHEESE GOUGERES

Gougeres are traditional savoury choux pastries. They're very light but have a lovely cheesy flavour which makes them the perfect accompaniment to drinks.

Ingredients: ***(makes 36)***

250ml water
65g cold butter, cut into small cubes
125g plain flour
1 teaspoon dry mustard powder
4 eggs
100g Gruyère cheese, finely grated
Sea salt and black pepper
Milk for glazing
1 teaspoon paprika

Method:

Pre-heat the oven to 180°C/Gas 4.

Sieve together the mustard and flour.

Bring the water and butter to the boil in a heavy-based saucepan, then remove from the heat and tip in all the flour and mustard in one go. Mix with a wooden spoon for about a minute or until the mixture comes away from the sides of the pan.

Next beat in 2 of the eggs and when thoroughly incorporated beat in the remaining 2. Finally beat in ⅔ of the grated cheese and season well.

Line a baking sheet with non-stick baking paper and, working with two wet teaspoons, shape the mixture into small balls about the size of a walnut, spacing well to allow for expansion.

Bake for about 15 minutes or until well risen and golden brown. Brush each one with a drop of milk and sprinkle with the remaining cheese.

Serve dusted with a little paprika.

Tip: The mixture can be made an hour or so ahead of time but the gougeres are best served hot from the oven.

MERLOT

after dark

BEER-BATTERED OYSTERS WITH A SHOT OF BLOODY MARY

This is an excellent way to introduce oysters to people who might otherwise shy away from them.

Ingredients: ***(makes 12)***

12 freshly-shucked oysters, shells reserved and boiled for 3 minutes to clean

A little plain flour for dusting

100g self-raising flour

150ml lager

Salt and freshly milled pepper

Vegetable oil for frying

Rock salt to serve

For the Bloody Mary:

500ml 'Clamato' juice or failing this, regular tomato juice

6 shots of best quality vodka

2 teaspoons freshly grated horseradish

Juice of 1 lemon

Dash of Worcester sauce

Dash of Tabasco

Fresh black pepper

Celery sticks to garnish

Method:

Mix the Bloody Mary ingredients together in a large jug and chill.

Heat the oil in a heavy-based pan to approximately 180°C or until a cube of bread sizzles when dropped in it.

Place the self-raising flour in a bowl and whisk in the lager until you have a smooth batter. Season well.

Dredge each oyster in a little plain flour and then coat well in the batter.

Carefully lower the battered oysters into the hot oil and fry for a couple of minutes on each side or until light, puffy and golden brown – do not overcook. You will probably have to do this in two batches. Drain on paper towels and set aside in a warm place while you pour the Bloody Marys.

On a serving tray, place the reserved oyster shells on little beds of rock salt next to a shot of Bloody Mary, put the hot battered oysters back in their shells and serve.

TIP: To shuck fresh oysters wet a tea towel and wring it out. Hold the rounded part of the oyster in the cloth and insert either an oyster knife or more likely a normal round-ended dinner knife into the join between the shells. With a firm grip apply some pressure until you feel them coming apart and then twist to open. Gently tease away the muscle that joins the oyster to the shell and you're off!

SEARED SIRLOIN OF BEEF WITH WASABI DIP

This came to me while eating good old fashioned roast beef and horseradish and is really just a 'Japanesey' twist on that. It's a great one to do ahead of time as the steak is marinated beforehand and really keeps its flavour when served cold. Try a glass of chilled sake with it.

Ingredients: *(makes 24)*

For the beef:

2 sirloin steaks, each about 2.5cm thick and weighing approximately 250g

2 tablespoons light soy sauce

1 tablespoon rice vinegar

1 tablespoon mirin (sweetened sake used for cooking)

2 teaspoons sesame oil

For the dip:

1 cup mayonnaise

½ tablespoon wasabi paste (more if you like it hot)

1 tablespoon rice vinegar

1 tablespoon mirin

Method:

Trim away any visible fat from the edges of the steaks and place in a shallow non-metallic container.

Mix together the marinade ingredients and pour over the steaks. You now marinate the steak for anything up to 12 hours, but 1 hour will do.

Pre-heat a ridged grill pan until it's very hot.

Sear the steaks for a couple of minutes on each side so that they're still pink in the middle. Set aside and allow to cool.

With a very sharp knife cut the steaks into thin slices across the grain and thread onto bamboo skewers.

Finally, whisk together the dip ingredients and place in a bowl surrounded by the beef and serve.

MONKFISH, CHORIZO AND ROSEMARY SPIEDINI WITH SMOKED PAPRIKA AIOLI

I love the taste combination of the smoky chorizo and firm-fleshed monkfish, tinged with rosemary. These are absolutely delicious with a glass of chilled sherry.

Ingredients: *(makes 24)*

24 rosemary branches about 8cm long

350g monkfish tail, skinned, boned and cut into 2.5cm cubes

350g cooking chorizo, cut into similar sized chunks as the monkfish

Olive oil, salt and pepper

1 quantity of smoked paprika aioli (see Basics)

Method:

Pre-heat the grill or barbecue.

To make the rosemary skewers pull the leaves off the stalks leaving just a few at one end.

Drop the skewers into a bowl of water and allow to soak for 10 minutes. (This will stop them from burning when the spiedini are grilled).

Thread the monkfish onto the skewers, followed by the chorizo.

Place on a baking tray, brush with olive oil, season with salt and pepper and put under the grill (or on the barbecue) for 2–3 minutes on each side.

Serve warm with the aioli.

MINI BAKED POTATOES WITH CRÈME FRAÎCHE AND CAVIAR

This is not so much a recipe as a call to arms. The combination of hot little potatoes, creamy crème fraîche and lavish amounts of caviar is a classic one and quite simply sublime. The purist in me wants to extol the virtues of using only the best Oscietra Gold caviar but the pragmatist in me feels duty bound to tell you that I often use Avruga, which is as cheap as chips by comparison and available in most good supermarkets.

Ingredients: ***(makes 24)***

24 small new potatoes as even in shape as possible

200ml crème fraîche (not half fat!)

55g jar of the best caviar you can afford

Method:

Pre-heat the oven to 200°C/Gas 6.

Wash the potatoes, place on a baking tray and roast in the oven for approximately 20 minutes. Keep an eye on them as the time varies according to the type of potato.

When they're cooked, remove from the oven and allow to cool. When completely cool, scoop out a small hollow in each with a melon-baller or teaspoon (if they refuse to sit neatly, slice a tiny bit off the bottom to level).

Place the crème fraîche in a disposable piping bag (this makes filling the potatoes much easier and quicker) and have the caviar at the ready.

Just before serving, put the potatoes back in the oven for a couple of minutes to reheat them. When hot, quickly pipe a bit of crème fraîche into each hollow and top with caviar. Place on a platter and serve at once.

LOBSTER, CRÈME FRAÎCHE AND TARRAGON VOL AU VENTS

These have to be the poshest vol au vents ever! They are a real special occasion treat and never disappoint. The delicate filling is bound together with tangy crème fraîche worlds apart from the watery prawn vol au vents of my youth. You can make your own cases as I have done or you could track down some good quality ready-made ones.

Ingredients: ***(makes 12)***

1 pack (2 sheets) of ready-rolled puff pastry

200g cooked lobster meat (1 x 600g cooked lobster or 1 large cooked lobster tail will yield roughly this amount of picked meat)

4 tablespoons full fat crème fraîche

2 tablespoons fresh tarragon, chopped

Zest of a lemon, finely grated

Egg yolk, beaten for glazing

Salt and pepper

Method:

Pre-heat the oven to 180°C/Gas 6.

On a floured surface cut out 12 squares of pastry measuring 5cm x 5cm. With the tip of a sharp knife score a line 1cm in from the edge being careful not to cut all the way through.

Place on a baking tray lined with non-stick paper and bake in a pre-heated oven for 5 minutes. Take out of the oven and with the tip of a knife remove the middle of the vol au vents to create a cavity. Brush them with egg yolk and return to the oven for a further 5–10 minutes until crisp and golden brown.

To make the filling, chop the lobster meat into small pieces and add the crème fraîche, tarragon, lemon zest, salt and pepper. When the vol au vent cases are perfectly cooled, fill and serve.

TIP: If you can't find lobster meat or fancy a slightly more inexpensive option, substitute cooked tiger prawns for the lobster meat or even half and half. You can fill the vol au vents up to 30 minutes before you want to serve them but the filling can be made up to 12 hours ahead.

BABY AUBERGINES STUFFED WITH COUS-COUS, YOGHURT AND HARISSA

I found these baby aubergines in my local Middle Eastern food shop and thought they'd make a fabulous little receptacle for a spicy cous-cous salad. The aubergines, when roasted whole, take on a delicious smokey taste which complements all the other Middle Eastern flavours in the filling. I think it's quite important to serve these at room temperature – if served chilled they'd lose almost all the delicate flavours and served hot they'd fail to hold their shape, promising to make an unholy mess!

Ingredients: ***(makes 24)***

12 baby aubergines

1 cup cous-cous

1 bunch each of mint, coriander and flat leaf parsley

2 cloves garlic, crushed

1–2 red chillies (depending on taste), de-seeded and finely chopped

100ml extra virgin olive oil

1 quantity yoghurt and harissa sauce (see Basics)

Method:

Pre-heat the oven to 180°C/Gas 6.

Lightly oil the aubergines and prick them a couple of times with the tip of a sharp knife to prevent them bursting in the oven. Place on a baking tray and bake for 12–15 minutes or until very soft and easily pierced with a knife. Allow to cool.

Mix the cous-cous with just enough boiling water to cover it and leave to stand for 5 minutes before fluffing up with a fork. Place the herbs, garlic, chilli and olive oil in a processor and blend to a paste. Season with salt and pepper and stir into the cous-cous.

Make a slit in the aubergines and scoop out a little pulp to make room for the stuffing. Add the aubergine pulp to the cous-cous and pile back into the shells. Place onto a serving tray.

Dollop a little yoghurt and harissa sauce onto each aubergine just before serving.

INDIVIDUAL CAESAR SALADS

This is possibly everyone's favourite salad and what could be better than getting a whole one to yourself? Packed with lots of authentic caesar salad flavour these are light but surprisingly filling, so count on no more than 2 each if you're offering other nibbles.

Ingredients: ***(makes 24)***

Dressing:

1 cup good quality mayonnaise
1 clove garlic, crushed
3 tablespoons finely-grated Parmesan
2 teaspoons Worcestershire sauce
1 tablespoon fresh lemon juice
Salt and pepper

Salad:

4–6 little gem lettuces
12 hard-boiled quail eggs, each cut in half
6 anchovy fillets, each split into 4
1 cup stale white bread, cut into small cubes
Bunch of chives, cut into 1cm lengths
Extra Parmesan for shaving
Vegetable oil for frying

Method:

Make the dressing by whisking together all the ingredients and if it's a touch thick add a little cold water. Set aside.

Make the croutons by heating a couple of tablespoons of vegetable oil in a heavy frying pan or wok until hot but not smoking. Add the cubes of bread and stir fry until golden brown and crispy. Drain on a paper towel and allow to cool.

Cut the base of each little gem and with your hands pull away each layer of leaves. When you have done this to all of them, select 24 of the best-looking leaves and set aside.

Finely shred the remaining leaves and combine in a bowl with just enough of the dressing to bind together.

Place the reserved leaves on a serving platter and top with the dressed, shredded leaves. Top each salad with half a quail's egg, crouton and anchovy fillet. Finish with an extra drizzle of dressing, a sprinkle of chives and a shaving of Parmesan. Serve immediately.

TIP: The dressing can be made a day in advance and kept in the fridge. You may find however that it thickens slightly overnight; this is normal, simply thin it with a little cold water. The rest of the salads must be done just before you need them otherwise the lettuce will discolour.

BROCCOLI AND BLUE CHEESE WON TONS WITH PLUM SAUCE

When I first came across this dish many years ago I thought it sounded like a very peculiar combination. At the time it was very much the fashion to cook 'East meets West' type food and for most of that period the result was pretty disgusting! However, when you think about it, all the elements of this dish are pure classics: broccoli and blue cheese, blue cheese and fruit, won tons and plum sauce. They all go together really well and have understandably survived the test of time to become a firm favourite of mine.

Ingredients: *(makes 24)*

24 fresh won ton wrappers, thawed if frozen (available from Asian supermarkets)

2 large heads of broccoli

250g blue cheese such as Stilton or Gorgonzola

Salt and pepper

Vegetable oil, for frying

Plum sauce, to serve

Method:

Separate the broccoli into florets and thinly slice the stems. Steam for about 7 minutes or until the broccoli is cooked through. Allow to cool and when completely cold mash with a fork and crumble in the cheese. The mixture should still have some texture to it.

Working with 6 won ton wrappers at a time, place them in a row on a clean, dry work surface. Put a teaspoon of the filling in the middle of each and dampen the edges with a wet finger. Now simply gather up the corners and twist into a 'money bag' shape.

Place the won tons on a tray lined with baking parchment and refrigerate until you are ready to fry and serve them.

Put the vegetable oil in a heavy-bottomed frying pan or wok to a depth of about 2.5cm. Alternatively use an electric deep fat frier if you have one. Heat the oil to approximately 190°C or until a cube of bread sizzles and turns golden brown in 10 seconds.

Fry the won tons, in batches if necessary, until golden brown. Drain on kitchen paper and season with salt and pepper.

Serve piled high with a dipping bowl of the plum sauce.

CHICKEN, CHILLI AND CORIANDER QUASADILLAS

Quasadillas (pronounced 'kay-sad-eeyas') are basically cheesey Mexican sandwiches. In Mexico they're often not much more than flour tortillas filled with cheese and fried, but here I've given them a slightly more interesting filling and oven-baked them for a lighter taste.

Ingredients: ***(makes 24)***

4 flour tortillas
250g cooked chicken, shredded
250g mild Cheddar, grated
1 small red onion, thinly sliced
1 small bunch coriander, chopped
1 small red chilli, de-seeded and chopped (or more if you like it spicy)

Method:

Pre-heat the oven to 200°C/Gas 6.

Heat a ridged grill pan until very hot and grill each of the tortillas briefly on one side only, until nicely marked.

Mix the filling ingredients together in a bowl and then divide between 2 of the tortillas. Top with the remaining tortillas to make 2 'sandwiches' and press down firmly.

Put the 'sandwiches' on a baking sheet and place in the oven for 5 minutes or until the cheese is melted.

Cut each quasadilla into 12 and place on a serving plate.

TIP: The flour tortillas can be filled a day in advance and then baked in the oven when you need them.

BEETROOT-MARINATED SALMON WITH HORSERADISH AND SALMON CAVIAR

These elegant morsels are as much a feast for the eyes as they are for the palate – guaranteed to wow your guests! The method of semi-curing the salmon really helps the flavours penetrate the fish and the horseradish cuts through the sweetness beautifully. By serving these on Chinese soup spoons each person gets a perfectly contained portion of salmon.

Ingredients: *(makes 24)*

500g salmon fillet from the middle of the fish, skinned and pin boned

2 medium, raw beetroot, peeled and grated

4 tablespoons sugar

2 tablespoons sea salt

4 tablespoons hot horseradish sauce

50g 'Keta caviar' (otherwise known as salmon roe or salmon caviar)

Sprigs of dill, to garnish

Vegetable oil for frying

Method:

Place the salmon fillet in a non-metallic container. Mix the grated beetroot, salt and sugar and pour over the salmon. Mix well so that the fish is coated on both sides with the mixture. Place a plate on top and weigh down with a couple of tins from your cupboard.

Place in the fridge for 24 hours.

The following day, scrape the marinade off and rinse the salmon briefly under cold running water, then pat dry.

Heat a non-stick frying pan with a drop of vegetable oil and sear the salmon on each side for 1 minute. Remove and cool. With a very sharp knife cut the salmon into 2.5cm cubes and place on the Chinese soup spoons. Top with a small amount of horseradish, followed by a few beads of 'Keta' and a sprig of dill, and serve.

TIP: Only brief searing is required in this recipe due to the curing process, which partially 'cooks' the fish. If you prefer a more thoroughly-cooked piece of salmon, sear it for 2–3 minutes on each side.

feeding a crowd

SOUP SHOTS

The trick with these is to make sure there is plenty of flavour in the soups. You're only giving your guests a small amount so make sure they pack a punch!

Each makes 12 espresso cups:

SPINACH, GORGONZOLA AND BASIL SOUP

1 medium onion, sliced

1 finely-chopped clove of garlic

250g cleaned spinach leaves (the young ones sold pre-washed in bags are perfect for this)

100g Gorgonzola cheese

A bunch of basil

750ml good stock, chicken or vegetable

Fry the onion and garlic until soft, then add the stock and bring to the boil. Turn off the heat, add the spinach and stir through until wilted. Place in a processor with the cheese and basil and blend until smooth.

CARROT, ORANGE AND CARDAMOM SOUP

6 medium carrots, peeled and chopped

1 medium onion, sliced

2 cloves garlic, crushed

6 cardamom pods, crushed

500ml good stock, chicken or vegetable

250ml freshly-squeezed orange juice

Fry the onion, garlic and cardamom until soft. Then add the carrots and stock, and simmer for 20 minutes or until carrots are soft. Place in a processor with the orange juice and blend until as smooth as possible. Push through a medium sieve and return to the pan to keep warm.

BEETROOT, CUMIN AND GINGER SOUP

4 cooked beetroot, roughly chopped (use rubber gloves for this)

1 medium onion, sliced

2 cloves garlic, crushed

1 teaspoon cumin seeds, toasted in a dry pan and then crushed in a pestle and mortar

A piece of fresh ginger the size of your thumb, chopped or grated

750ml good stock, chicken or vegetable

2 tablespoons double cream

Salt and pepper

Fry the onion, garlic, cumin and ginger until soft. Add the beetroot and stock and then simmer for 5 minutes. Put in a processor and blend until really smooth. Add the cream and season with salt and pepper.

SESAME & SEAWEED CRUSTED TUNA

I'm passionate about tuna and when I find a piece that is fantastically fresh I'm loath to cook it for more than a few seconds. Unfortunately the kind of tuna you find in most supermarkets is rarely fresh enough and just wouldn't do for this kind of recipe. Instead, seek out a good fishmonger and ask for 'sashimi grade tuna'. Let them know that you plan to serve it raw. The sesame and seaweed seasoning in this recipe is often sold wherever you can buy sushi-making kits and adds a lovely savoury flavour to the tuna. If you can't track any down, simply use sesame seeds instead for an equally delicious variation.

Ingredients: ***(makes 24)***

500g sashimi grade yellow fin tuna, cut into 2.5cm steaks

4 tablespoons of 'Furikake' seasoning or plain sesame seeds

1 teaspoon toasted sesame oil

Dipping sauce:

200ml light soy sauce

100ml mirin

A few drops of toasted sesame oil

1 small red chilli, de-seeded and finely chopped

Small bunch of coriander, finely chopped

Method:

Make the dipping sauce by combining the ingredients and setting aside.

Evenly spread out the Furikake (or sesame seeds) onto a shallow plate. Rub the tuna steaks with a very small amount of sesame oil and then press each side onto the seasoning. Set aside.

Heat a non-stick frying pan until very hot, but do not add any oil. Sear the tuna steaks for 30 seconds on each side and remove to a tray to cool.

When completely cool, cut into small cubes with a very sharp knife. Arrange on a serving tray and skewer each one with a cocktail stick. Serve the dipping sauce alongside.

MINI SAUSAGES IN A SWEET AND STICKY GLAZE

These are without doubt the ultimate crowd pleaser. Simple and very, very moreish they're not so much a recipe as a suggestion. Try varying the flavours by using mini lamb sausages and glazing them with redcurrant jelly.

Ingredients: ***(makes 48)***

48 cocktail pork sausages
1 jar of good quality onion relish
1 tablespoon balsamic vinegar
1 tablespoon vegetable oil

Method:

Pre-heat the oven to 200°C/Gas 6.

Toss the sausages in the vegetable oil and then tip them into a baking dish. Cook for about 15 minutes giving them a good stir halfway through to ensure they all brown evenly.

When they're nice and golden brown add the onion relish and vinegar before returning to the oven for a further 5 minutes.

Serve hot in a big bowl with tooth picks handed round separately.

THAI SALAD OF PRAWNS AND PINK GRAPEFRUIT ON BETEL LEAVES

This fabulously tasty snack is based on one commonly sold by street vendors in Thailand known as 'Miang Lao'. The original is a rather complicated affair including tiny dried shrimps and salted turnips. This version is simpler and more of a tangy, refreshing salad. The actual leaves on which the salad is served are known as 'betel leaves' and can sometimes be ordered from Asian greengrocers, but if you can't find any use baby spinach leaves for an equally delicious alternative.

Ingredients: *(makes 24)*

24 betel leaves (or baby spinach leaves)
16 cooked, peeled and de-veined prawns, diced
½ red onion, cut into small dice
Small bunch coriander, chopped
2 pink grapefruit, segmented and diced
2 tablespoons roasted peanuts, chopped
1 tablespoon fresh ginger, peeled and finely diced
1 tablespoon of lime, finely diced (if you can, try to find the small thin-skinned Thai variety)

Dressing:

Juice of 2 limes
1 tablespoon Thai fish sauce
1 tablespoon sweet chilli sauce

Method:

Combine the dressing ingredients and set aside.

Mix all the other salad ingredients together, except the betel leaves.

Just before serving, dress the salad and place the betel leaves on a serving platter. Top each leaf with some salad and allow the guests to fold them into little parcels before eating.

TIP: To de-vein a prawn, make a shallow slit along its back and hold under cold running water to wash away any impurities.

PISSALADIERE

This variation of the Provençal classic makes a fantastic alternative to the more traditional pizza. Roughly cut into bite-sized pieces and serve at room temperature.

Ingredients: ***(makes 24)***

1 quantity of basic bread dough, allowed to rise and knocked back (see Basics)

2 tins of chopped tomatoes

2 garlic cloves, crushed

2 tablespoons olive oil

2 large onions, finely sliced

Fresh thyme

24 pitted black olives

12 anchovies in oil, drained and halved lengthways

Method:

Pre-heat oven to 200°C/Gas 6.

To make the tomato sauce, heat one tablespoon of olive oil and fry the garlic for a couple of minutes. Add the tomatoes, simmer for 45 minutes until thick and reduced slightly. This can be done ahead of time.

Fry the onions in the other tablespoon of oil until soft and light golden brown – about 10 minutes.

Oil a large flat baking tray and roll out the bread dough thinly to fit the tray. Trim off any surplus and discard.

Thinly spread the tomato sauce over the pastry and top with the onions. Finally, lay the anchovies over in a sort of cross-hatch pattern and place an olive in each square. Scatter over with fresh thyme and bake for 15–20 minutes.

Roughly cut into bite-sized pieces and serve at room temperature.

GOUJONS OF DUCK WITH HOI SIN LIME SAUCE

These tasty little bites have a delicious flavour reminiscent of Peking duck but with the advantage of serving the meat still pink in the middle. The rather unusual addition of lime juice to the hoi sin makes them slightly less cloying, which means you can eat more of them!

Ingredients: ***(makes 24)***

2 large skinless duck breasts each cut into 12 thin slices
1 cup dried white breadcrumbs
2 tablespoons sesame seeds
1 cup plain flour
2 teaspoons Chinese 5 spice
3 eggs, beaten
Sea salt
Vegetable oil
1 cup hoi sin lime sauce (see Basics)

Method:

First of all, mix the sesame seeds and breadcrumbs, then place in a shallow container such as a Tupperware box.

Sieve the flour and the 5 spice into another shallow container, then put the beaten eggs in a third container.

Toss the strips of duck first in the flour mixture, then the egg mixture, followed by the breadcrumbs and sesame mix.

Space the goujons (for that is now what they are) well apart on a tray lined with some cling film or baking parchment and refrigerate for an hour.

Place the vegetable oil in a heavy-bottomed frying pan or wok, to a depth of about 2.5cm. Alternatively, use an electric deep fat frier if you have one. Heat the oil to approximately 190°C or until a cube of bread sizzles and turns golden brown in 10 seconds.

Fry the goujons, in batches if necessary, until golden brown and drain on kitchen paper. Season with sea salt and serve piled high with a bowl of the hoi sin lime sauce for dipping.

TIP: If you can't find good natural breadcrumbs try whizzing up a packet of plain breadsticks in a food processor for an excellent alternative.

PORK, LEMONGRASS AND CORIANDER SKEWERS

These make a great addition to any barbecue menu as when they're cooked over hot coals the flavour of the lemongrass skewers really penetrates the meat – delicious!

Ingredients: ***(makes 24)***

1kg minced pork

24 sticks lemongrass

2 tablespoons fish sauce

1 tablespoon ginger, grated

1 small bunch coriander, finely chopped

1–2 red chillies (according to taste), de-seeded and finely chopped

1 quantity of sweet chilli dip (see Basics)

Method:

Soak the lemongrass in cold water for 30 minutes – this will prevent the sticks from burning when on the grill.

Mix all the other ingredients in a large bowl until well combined.

Divide the mixture into 24 balls and mould around the middle of each lemongrass skewer like a kebab. Brush lightly with vegetable oil and cook on a barbecue (or very hot ridged grill pan) for about 5 minutes on each side or until cooked all the way through.

Serve with sweet chilli dip.

BROAD BEAN, PEA, FETA AND MINT FRITTATA

This may not seem an obvious choice for a miniature feast but it's absolutely delicious served at room temperature and cut into bite-sized pieces. In Italy, frittata is often served this way in *osterias* (the Italian name for an inn or wine bar), placed on the bar for people to enjoy with drinks.

Ingredients: ***(makes 24)***

12 free range eggs at room temperature

200g frozen broad beans, podded and skinned (see tip below)

200g frozen petit pois blanched for 2 minutes and refreshed in cold water

150g feta cheese cut into 2cm cubes

1 large onion, thinly sliced

2 cloves garlic, finely chopped

1 bunch mint, finely chopped

Olive oil

Salt and pepper

Method:

Pre-heat the oven to 180°C/Gas 4. Heat a little olive oil in an oven-friendly non-stick frying pan and sauté the onion and garlic until soft.

Lightly whisk the eggs with the salt and pepper and set aside. Add the podded broad beans and peas to the onion mix, then toss together. Add the eggs and mint, then with a wooden spoon draw in the edges of the frittata as they cook.

After about 5 minutes on a medium heat the bottom of the frittata will start to set. Remove the pan from the heat and scatter with the feta.

Place the pan in the pre-heated oven and bake for 12–15 minutes or until firm in the centre.

Turn out onto a chopping board and allow to cool. Cut into small bite-sized pieces and place a tooth pick in each. Arrange on a serving platter and serve at room temperature.

TIP: The easiest way to skin frozen broad beans is to plunge them into rapidly boiling water for 30 seconds and then straight into iced water. Between thumb and forefinger, gently squeeze the beans and they'll slip easily out of their skins.

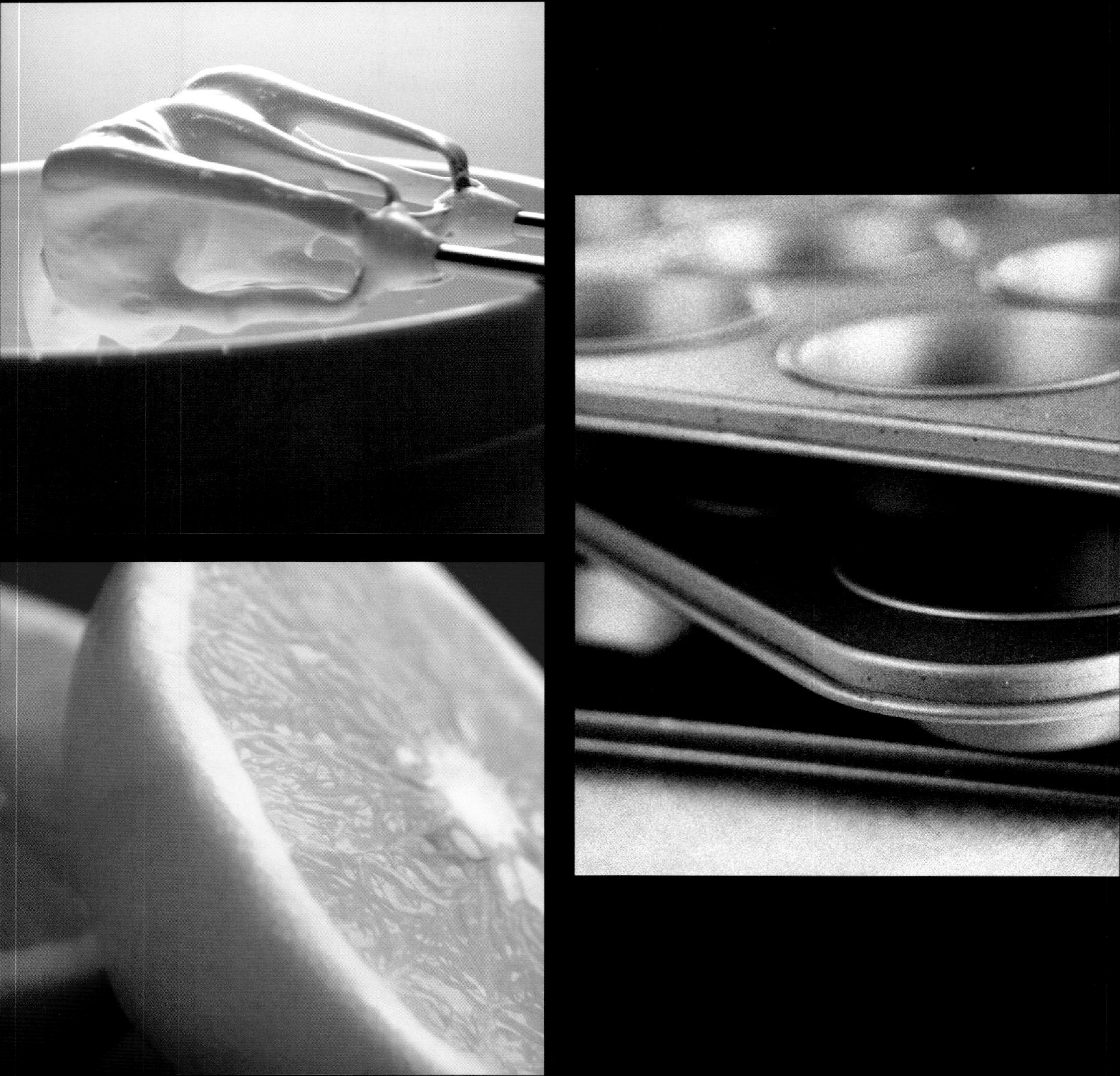

family favourites

MINI CORNISH PASTIES

I tried all sorts of variations of these miniature classics before being left in no doubt that the traditional filling simply cannot be improved upon – especially when served with good old fashioned ketchup for dipping. It's important when making pasties this size to cut the meat and vegetables quite small and of even sizes.

Ingredients: ***(makes 24)***

1 quantity shortcrust pastry (see Basics)
500g lean skirt of beef, diced
3 medium potatoes, peeled and diced
250g turnip, peeled and diced
Plenty of salt and pepper

Method:

Pre-heat the oven to 200°C/Gas 6.

Fry the meat and vegetables together in a large frying pan over a medium heat for about 5 minutes or until they take on a little colour. Set aside and allow to cool.

Roll out the pastry on a large floured surface to approximately 0.5cm thick. Using a 10cm biscuit cutter, cut out 24 disks in total, re-rolling the pastry as necessary.

Divide the filling between the discs, being careful not to overfill them. Brush the edges with a little water and then bring them up to meet in the middle before pinching in, as decoratively as you can, ensuring a good seal.

Place on an oven tray (or two) lined with baking parchment and bake for a total of 25 minutes, turning the oven down to 180°C/Gas 4 halfway through. Serve warm.

CORONATION CHICKEN ON MINI POPPADOMS

The original 'coronation chicken' was conceived in 1952 as part of a banquet to celebrate the coronation of Queen Elizabeth II. Ever since, it's been a popular buffet dish but like so many family favourites has lost its way over the years. This version has been given a new lease of life and is presented on mini poppadoms, which are a great vehicle for this spicy little number.

Ingredients: ***(makes 24)***

4 small cooked chicken breasts, cut into 1cm dice
1 small ripe mango, cut into 1cm dice
½ cup good quality mayonnaise
1 tablespoon medium curry powder
2 tablespoons toasted flaked almonds
2 tablespoons coriander, chopped
Salt and pepper
24 mini poppadoms
Vegetable oil for frying

Method:

Combine the chicken, mango, mayonnaise, curry powder and season. Set aside until ready to serve.

To cook the poppadoms, heat the vegetable oil to approximately 170°C in a heavy-based frying pan and fry the poppadoms in batches until light golden brown. They will take no more than a few seconds on each side. Drain on kitchen paper and allow to cool.

Just before you want to serve the poppadoms, stir the coriander into the chicken and mango mixture, then place a small amount onto each poppadom. Top with a few flaked almonds.

Arrange on a plate and serve.

TIP: To cook the chicken breasts, place them in a saucepan and cover with water. Bring to the boil, then reduce to a simmer and cook for 10–12 minutes. Turn off the heat and allow to cool in the water. You can make the coronation chicken up to 12 hours ahead but leave out the chopped coriander until the last minute.

BEANS ON TOAST

To give it its proper title, 'bruschetta con fagioli e pommodorini'. A delicious antipasto that's often found on the bar in *osterias* all over Italy, to be enjoyed for free with your drinks – it is, at the end of the day, posh beans on toast! Try to find a sour dough baguette as it does make a difference to the finished crostini.

Ingredients: *(makes 24)*

1 baguette, sour dough if possible
2 tins of cannellini beans, rinsed and drained
24 cherry tomatoes, halved
2 cloves garlic, cut in half
Extra virgin olive oil
A bunch of basil, torn roughly
Salt and pepper

Method:

Pre-heat a ridged grill pan.

Cut the baguette into 24 x 1cm slices and set aside.

Heat a tablespoon of olive oil in a frying pan and add the beans. Cook for about 5 minutes on a medium heat, add the tomatoes and then cook for a further 5 minutes or until the tomatoes start to break down slightly. Remove from heat and set aside. Add the torn basil, season with salt and pepper and keep warm.

To make the crostini, place the slices of bread on the grill pan and allow to toast well on each side. While the crostini are still hot from the grill, rub each one with the cut side of a garlic clove.

Top each crostini with some of the bean mixture and serve at room temperature.

INDIVIDUAL PRAWN COCKTAILS

The poor old prawn cocktail has had such bad press over the last couple of decades and not without good reason. Limp lettuce and watery frozen prawns were enough to put me off for years. Here though, each person is presented with an individual serving of crisp little gem lettuce and plump tiger prawns in a delicately spiced dressing. I've tried not to tinker with the original version too much, I've just used really fresh ingredients and updated the dressing a bit.

Ingredients: ***(makes 12)***

500g raw tiger prawns with the shell on (if frozen, defrost thoroughly)

4 little gem lettuces

Bunch spring onions, finely sliced

4 tablespoons mayonnaise

1 teaspoon tomato purée

1 tablespoon sweet chilli sauce

½ teaspoon Thai fish sauce

Juice ½ lime

12 pieces fresh banana leaf, cut into triangles measuring 15cm x 15cm x 20cm (optional)

Method:

First, cook the prawns by dropping into rapidly boiling salted water. Cook for 3 minutes and then cool under running water. Peel the prawns and de-vein.

Make the dressing by whisking together the mayonnaise, tomato purée, sweet chilli sauce, fish sauce and lime juice. Set aside.

Cut the base of each little gem and with your hands pull away each layer of leaves. When you've done this to all 4, select 12 of the best looking leaves and set aside.

Finely shred the remaining leaves into a bowl and combine with the prawns and just enough of the dressing to bind together.

If you're using the banana leaves, roll them into cones and secure with a tooth pick. Sit each cone in a shot glass and place a reserved lettuce leaf in each. If you're not using the banana leaves, arrange the lettuce straight into the shot glasses. Finally fill each cone with the prawn cocktail and garnish with spring onions. Serve on a tray with a wooden fork in each one.

CHILLI CON CARNE IN CORN CUPS

The question of how to serve chill con carne as finger food was a tricky one. However, that said, once an individual portion of spicy chilli is held in a little home-made corn cup any doubts are removed and the portable chilli is born! One word of caution though, make plenty of these as they are very popular!

Ingredients: *(makes 24)*

For the corn cups:

300g masa harina

250ml warm water

2 tablespoons olive oil

1 teaspoon salt

For the chilli:

250g lean minced beef

½ onion, finely chopped

1 tin chopped tomatoes

1 teaspoon toasted ground cumin

1 clove garlic, finely chopped

1 red chilli, de-seeded and finely chopped

1 400g tin kidney beans, rinsed and drained

1 teaspoon cocoa powder

Salt and pepper

To serve:

Sour cream and guacamole (see Basics)

Method:

Pre-heat the oven to 170°C/Gas 3.

Mix the dry corn cup ingredients in a large bowl and gradually add the water. You may need slightly more or less water, so add a little at a time. Knead to a smooth dough and rest for 30 minutes.

Divide the mixture into 24 small balls and working in two batches press pieces of the dough into each indentation of a 12-hole mini muffin tin until you have a cup shape. Bake for 10–12 minutes and repeat with the rest of the dough. Allow to cool on a wire rack.

Make the chilli by frying off the onion, garlic and spices, followed by the minced beef. When the meat is browned add the tomatoes & cocoa and simmer for 35 minutes. Finish by adding the beans and season well.

To serve, fill the corn cups with chilli and top with guacamole and sour cream – serve hot.

TIP: The corn cups will keep for a week in an airtight container. Masa harina is flour made from ground, dried corn kernels and can be found wherever Mexican ingredients are sold. While it is essential to this recipe, if you can't find it, you could serve your chilli on shop-bought corn chips.

MOROCCAN SPICED LAMB SAUSAGE ROLLS

These are a delicious twist on the more traditional pork sausage rolls and are small enough to justify eating quite a few!

Ingredients: ***(makes 24)***

500g lamb and mint sausages

50g fresh white breadcrumbs

1 teaspoon harrissa paste

1 teaspoon cumin seeds, fried in a dry pan and then crushed in a pestle and mortar

½ teaspoon ground cinnamon

1 pack of ready-rolled puff pastry at room temperature (most brands contain two sheets)

1 egg yolk, lightly beaten

Salt and pepper

To serve:

Yoghurt and harissa dipping sauce (See Basics)

Method:

Pre-heat the oven to 200°C/Gas 6.

Slit the sausage skins and squeeze the filling into a large bowl.

Add the harissa paste, cumin, cinnamon, breadcumbs and salt and pepper. Mix well and set aside.

On a floured surface open out the puff pastry and cut each sheet in half lengthways, leaving you with four long rectangles.

Divide the filling into four and roll each quarter into a long sausage to fit the length of the pastry.

Brush the edges with water and roll up each one into a cylinder, pressing the edges to seal well. With a serrated knife cut each roll into 6 and place on a baking sheet lined with silicone paper.

Brush with the beaten egg and bake for 12–15 minutes or until nicely golden brown.

Serve at room temperature with yoghurt and harissa dipping sauce.

LITTLE SHEPHERD'S PIES TOPPED WITH LANCASHIRE CHEESE MASH

As the main contender for the ultimate comfort food, I was determined to get a miniature version of shepherd's pie in here somehow! These are fairly traditional apart from the fact they're topped with a cheesy mash and encased in a pastry shell, making them perfect for parties where everybody can have their very own pie all to themselves!

Ingredients: ***(makes 12)***

½ quantity of shortcrust pastry (see Basics)
250g lean minced lamb (definitely not beef)
1 small onion, finely chopped
1 medium carrot, peeled and finely chopped
1 tablespoon vegetable oil
1 tablespoon tomato purée
½ lamb stock cube
Pinch fresh rosemary, finely chopped
Salt and pepper
4 large potatoes, peeled, quartered, boiled and mashed with a little milk
100gm Lancashire cheese, crumbled

Method:

Pre-heat oven to 180°C/Gas 4.

Heat the oil in a large frying pan and fry the onion and carrot until slightly soft. Add the lamb and continue to sauté until browned before adding the tomato purée and crumbling in the lamb stock cube. At this stage the mixture will be a little too thick, so add a couple of tablespoons of water – just enough to loosen it as you don't want the mixture to be sloppy.

Check for seasoning and add the rosemary. Set aside to cool.

While the mixture is cooling, roll out the pastry to a thickness of about 0.5cm and using a 10cm pastry cutter cut out 12 discs. Gently press the discs into a greased 12-hole Yorkshire pudding tin. Trim away any excess pastry to give a neat edge. Chill the tray for 10 minutes.

Half-fill each pastry case with the lamb mixture and then fork over some mashed potato, making sure you completely cover the meat. Sprinkle a little cheese onto each.

Place in the centre of the oven for approximately 30 minutes, keeping an eye on them to ensure they don't brown too much.

When cooked, allow to cool slightly before easing out of the tin and placing on a serving platter.

CRAB CAKES WITH SPICY PINEAPPLE SALSA

A twist on the fish cakes of my youth, these are a spicier, more grown-up version. Picked white crab meat is available in pasteurised vacuum packs and is perfect for this recipe but you must double check for small pieces of shell.

Ingredients: ***(makes 12)***

150g picked white crab meat
1 cup of cold mashed potatoes (about 1 large potato)
1 tablespoon coriander, finely chopped
Salt and pepper
2 eggs, beaten
½ cup plain flour
½ cup dried white natural breadcrumbs
Vegetable oil

For the salsa:

¼ fresh pineapple, peeled and finely chopped
1 red chilli, de-seeded and finely chopped
½ red onion, finely chopped
Juice ½ lime
Sea salt and pepper

Method:

Mix together the crab meat, potato, coriander and seasoning. Then divide into 12 small patties.

Place the flour into a shallow container such as a Tupperware box. Take 2 more shallow containers and do the same with the beaten egg and breadcrumbs. Toss the crab cakes first in the flour, then the egg, followed by the breadcrumbs and set aside on a tray in the fridge, uncovered for a minimum of 30 minutes.

Combine the salsa ingredients and set aside.

To cook the crab cakes pour the oil into a heavy-based frying pan to a depth of about 1cm and heat to approximately 170°C or until a piece of bread sizzles and browns in 15 seconds.

Fry the crab cakes until golden brown on each side (by which time they will be hot in the middle) and serve on tooth picks or skewered onto forks with the salsa alongside for dipping.

TIP: The fish cakes can be made and coated in the breadcrumbs up to 24 hours ahead of time and refrigerated until you need them.

BREAD

something sweet

INDIVIDUAL RASPBERRY AND PASSIONFRUIT TRIFLES

A suitably indulgent way to end an evening of savoury grazing. The best thing about these little trifles is that they rely solely on shop-bought ingredients, but are delicious for it nonetheless.

Ingredients: ***(makes 12)***

3 slices shop-bought plain sponge cake
100ml sweet white wine
50ml crème de framboise (raspberry liqueur)
250g fresh raspberries
250ml fresh custard (shop-bought)
250g tub mascarpone
1 tablespoon icing sugar
3 passionfruit

Method:

Cut the cake into 1cm cubes and place in the bottom of 12 shot glasses. Mix the wine and liqueur before drizzling over the cake so that it's moist but not soaked.

Divide the raspberries between the glasses followed by the custard.

Next, whisk the mascarpone with the icing sugar and dollop on top of the trifles.

Refrigerate for 1 hour and just before serving cut open the passionfruits and squeeze out the juice into a small bowl.

Spoon a little passionfruit pulp over each trifle and serve with teaspoons alongside.

Tip: You can vary the alcohol in the trifles to suit your own taste. Try sherry, marsala or even ginger wine.

GRILLED PINEAPPLE WITH HOT CHOCOLATE FONDUE

Not fondue in the truest sense of the word, but the combination of the sweet pineapple and dark chocolate is a winner.

Ingredients: *(makes 24)*

For the fondue:

2 cups dark brown sugar

2 tablespoons cocoa powder

75g unsalted butter

1 cup double cream

For the grilled pineapple:

1 small ripe pineapple, peeled, cored and cut into bite-sized chunks

2 tablespoons of icing sugar

Method:

Pre-heat the grill to its highest setting.

Bring all the fondue ingredients up to the boil in a heavy-based saucepan. Simmer for 5 minutes, stirring constantly to help prevent any sticking. Keep warm.

Lay the pineapple pieces on an ovenproof tray and pat off any excess moisture with kitchen paper. Dust the chunks with icing sugar and grill for a few minutes until they start to caramelise at the edges.

Thread onto skewers and serve with the chocolate fondue.

AZTEC BROWNIES

These little brownies are a fantastic finale to end a party with. They're so rich and scrumptious that the addition of chilli and spices tends to creep up on people slowly. The chilli and chocolate combination is, of course, an ancient one and done with a light hand is quite sublime. I have placed some real gold leaf (which is totally edible) on top of mine just to reinforce the name – if you fancy doing the same you can buy it from good artists' suppliers. Very carefully brush the tops of the brownies with a little water and then gently press the gold leaf on top – as simple as that!

Ingredients: ***(makes 24)***

180g best quality dark chocolate (no less than 70% cocoa solids)

180g unsalted butter

250g dark muscovado sugar

3 eggs, beaten

100g plain flour

1 teaspoon ground cinnamon

½ teaspoon ground ginger

Pinch ground cloves

Pinch ground nutmeg

1 teaspoon dried chilli flakes

Method:

Pre-heat the oven to 180°C/Gas 4.

In a large heatproof bowl melt together the chocolate and butter. This can be done in the traditional way over simmering water or more conveniently in a microwave at 1-minute intervals at full power.

In a separate bowl whisk together the sugar and eggs. Then add the chocolate mixture to the sugar and eggs, mixing thoroughly. Sieve together the flour and spices and stir into the chocolate mixture.

Turn into a shallow baking tray measuring approximately 20cm x 30cm x 5cm, lined with baking parchment, and bake for 15-20 minutes.

When ready (it should still be squidgey in the middle when tested with a toothpick), cool in the tin and then cut into small squares.

Tip: If you don't have a tray with the exact measurements suggested above, don't worry: so long as it is roughly that size, your brownies will be fine. If it's a little smaller, they'll be deeper brownies and if the tin is a little bigger, well, you get the idea.

MINI BAKED ALASKA

The combination of crisp filo pastry, frozen ice cream and hot meringue really impresses in this reworking of a classic dessert. Don't worry about the ice cream melting as the meringue will protect it and, apart from anything else, it doesn't have time to melt as these disappear off the tray so quickly! You will need a small kitchen blow torch for this recipe as working on this scale prohibits you from putting them in a hot oven, as is traditional.

Ingredients: ***(makes 12)***
3 sheets of filo pastry
50g unsalted butter, melted
½ litre best quality vanilla ice cream
2 egg whites
75g caster sugar

Method:

Place a metal tray lined with baking parchment in the freezer. To prepare the ice cream use a melon baller to scoop out 12 balls and place onto the tray, cover with cling film and return to the freezer, preferably overnight.

Pre-heat the oven to 150°C/Gas 2.

To make the filo baskets, brush one sheet of filo with melted butter and place another sheet on top. Repeat this with the third sheet, being sure to brush the top layer with butter. Cut 12 squares of pastry measuring approximately 8cm x 8cm and press one into each hole of a 12-hole mini muffin tin. Bake for 8–10 minutes or until crisp and golden. Cool completely.

To make the meringue, beat the egg whites with an electric whisk until stiff peaks form and then, still beating, gradually add the caster sugar. Beat until very stiff and glossy.

To serve, put a ball of ice cream into each filo basket and quickly top with some meringue, making sure the ice cream is completely covered. Light your blow torch and carefully glaze the top of each meringue until they're a lovely golden brown colour, then serve at once.

Tip: An extra pair of hands is really useful for this recipe. One of you can top the alaskas with meringue while the other glazes them with the blowtorch.

FROZEN VODKA SHOTS WITH FRUIT SALAD

Not your usual kind of fruit salad! This is actually something I have served in between the savoury items on a menu where it acts as a sort of boozy sorbet – either way they always go down well with an 'adult' crowd.

Ingredients: ***(makes 12)***

½ cantaloupe melon
½ honeydew melon
¼ small watermelon
12 shots vodka

Method:

With a melon baller scoop out 12 balls from each melon and thread three balls onto each wooden skewer.

Place each 'kebab' into a shot glass. Carefully pour a shot of vodka onto each and place on a tray.

Put the tray into the freezer for 1 hour until icy-cold and serve immediately.

Tip: Try substituting ripe papaya for the watermelon if it's out of season.

basics

SMOKED PAPRIKA AIOLI

Ingredients: ***(makes 1 cup)***
1 teaspoon Dijon mustard
2 egg yolks
2 peeled and chopped garlic cloves
1 teaspoon sherry vinegar
1 teaspoon smoked paprika
1 cup light olive oil
Pinch of sea salt

Method:
Blend all the ingredients (except the oil) in a food processor until smooth.

With the motor running, add the oil a few drops at a time until the aioli is the consistency of thick mayonnaise.

Remove and store in the fridge for up to 24 hours.

GUACAMOLE

Ingredients: ***(makes 1 cup)***
1 large ripe avocado
125ml sour cream
Juice of 1 lime
1 clove garlic, crushed
Salt and pepper

Method:
Peel the avocado and remove the stone and reserve for later. Purée all the ingredients in a food processor until smooth.

Remove to a plastic container and place the stone in the middle of it. This will help prevent the guacamole from discolouring.

Press cling film onto the surface and refrigerate for up to 4 hours.

YOGHURT AND HARISSA SAUCE

Ingredients: ***(makes 1 cup)***
1 cup strained Greek yoghurt
1–2 teaspoons harissa paste
1 tablespoon finely chopped coriander root
1 teaspoon lemon juice
Sea salt and pepper

Method:
Mix together until smooth and store in fridge for up to 24 hours.

HOI SIN LIME SAUCE

Chinese hoi sin sauce is one of those few things that's nearly impossible to make at home with any level of success. Do, however, look for a good brand that contains no monosodium glutamate or other nasties.

Ingredients: ***(makes 1 cup)***
1 cup hoi sin sauce
Juice of 1 lime
A pinch of Chinese 5 spice

Method:
Mix thoroughly and store in an airtight jar in the fridge for up to a week.

BASIC BREAD DOUGH

Ingredients: ***(makes about 500g)***
300g strong white bread flour
1 sachet easy blend yeast
1 teaspoon sugar
1½ teaspoons sea salt
1 tablespoon olive oil
Up to 200ml tepid water

Method:
Dissolve the sugar and yeast in half the water and allow to become frothy (about 10 minutes). Sieve the flour into a large bowl and add the frothy yeasted water. Mix well and add the olive oil. At this stage the dough will be a bit dry and raggedy but this is correct.

Cover and rest for 20 minutes. After 20 minutes add the salt and start to add the rest of the tepid water. Stop when you have a soft but not sticky dough. Knead the dough with the heel of your hand, turning it as you go. Continue for about 10 minutes or until the dough is shiny, smooth and elastic.

Cover with a tea towel and allow to rise somewhere warm for about 1½ hours. It should double in size in this time. Finally, when the dough has risen sufficiently, knock it back with a swift punch to deflate it. The dough is now ready to use.

N.B. The amount of water you need will always vary according to the type of flour you use and the temperature and humidity of the kitchen, so always add the water in stages and be prepared not to use all the water stated.

SHORTCRUST PASTRY

Ingredients: ***(makes about 375g)***
250g plain flour
125g cold butter cut into cubes
¼ teaspoon sea salt
2–3 tablespoons iced water

Method:
Sieve the flour and salt into a large bowl and add the butter.

Rub the butter into the flour with your fingertips until it is the consistency of breadcrumbs.

Add the water a tablespoon at a time and mix with a fork until it starts to come together into a ball.

Give it a final and brief knead, wrap in cling film and refrigerate for 1 hour before using.

SWEET CHILLI DIP

Ingredients: ***(makes 1 cup)***
1 cup crème fraîche
2 tablespoons sweet chilli sauce
1 clove garlic, very finely chopped
1 teaspoon Thai fish sauce
Sea salt and pepper

Method:
Mix together until smooth and store in fridge for up to 24 hours.